S0-AFD-485

Feb 18

Geckos

Kate Riggs

CREATIVE EDUCATION
CREATIVE PAPERBACKS

seedlings

Published by Creative Education and Creative Paperbacks
P.O. Box 227, Mankato, Minnesota 56002
Creative Education and Creative Paperbacks
are imprints of The Creative Company
www.thecreativecompany.us

Design by Ellen Huber; production by Joe Kahnke
Art direction by Rita Marshall
Printed in China

Photographs by Alamy (Vince Burton, Craig Ellenwood, Matthijs
Kuijpers), Dreamstime (Elfhandalie, Isselee), iStockphoto (defun,
pelooyen, stevesm, Svetlanistaya), Minden Pictures (Jabruson,
Chris Mattison, Robert Valentic), National Geographic Creative
(JOEL SARTORE, NATIONAL GEOGRAPHIC PHOTO ARK),
Shutterstock (Papa Bravo, Butterfly Hunter, Eric Isselee, Daimond
Shutter, mlorenz, Susan Schmitz), SuperStock (Biosphoto, Minden
Pictures)

Library of Congress Cataloging-in-Publication Data
Names: Riggs, Kate, author.
Title: Geckos / Kate Riggs.
Series: Seedlings.
Includes index.
Summary: A kindergarten-level introduction to geckos,
covering their growth process, behaviors, the varied climates
they call home, and such defining features as their gripping toes.
Identifiers: LCCN 2016054473 / ISBN 978-1-60818-868-0
(hardcover) / ISBN 978-1-62832-483-9 (pbk) / ISBN 978-1-
56660-916-6 (eBook)

Subjects: LCSH: Geckos—Juvenile literature.
Classification: LCC QL666.L245 R55 2017 / DDC 597.95/2—dc23

CCSS: RI.K.1, 2, 3, 4, 5, 6, 7;
RI.1.1, 2, 3, 4, 5, 6, 7; RF.K.1, 3; RF.1.1

First Edition HC 9 8 7 6 5 4 3 2 1
First Edition PBK 9 8 7 6 5 4 3 2 1

TABLE OF CONTENTS

Hello, Geckos! 5

Warm-Weather Living 7

Scaly Skin 8

Colors and Tails 10

Time to Eat! 12

Gecko Hatchlings 14

What Do Geckos Do? 16

Goodbye, Geckos! 18

Picture a Gecko 20

Words to Know 22

Read More 23

Websites 23

Index 24

Hello, geckos!

Warm-weather geckos are lizards. They live all around the world. But no geckos live in Antarctica.

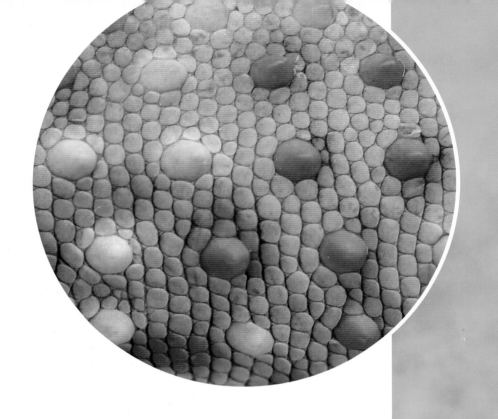

Geckos have soft, bumpy skin. It is covered in small, rounded scales.

The skin sheds as the gecko grows.

Geckos can be
many colors.

They have
a tail. It can
break off from
the body! Then
it grows back.

Geckos eat bugs. They eat other small animals, too.

Some geckos eat fruit.

A baby gecko is a hatchling. It comes out of an egg.

It must find its own
food right away.

Geckos climb trees with their sticky toes.

They hide on the leaves.
They wait for food.

Goodbye, geckos!

Picture a Gecko

tail

leg

scales

eye

foot

toe pad

Antarctica: a big piece of land covered with ice and snow

scales: small, thin plates covering the skin of lizards

Read More

Marsh, Laura. *Lizards.*
Washington, D.C.: National Geographic, 2012.

Riggs, Kate. *Geckos.*
Mankato, Minn.: Creative Education, 2015.

Websites

National Geographic Kids: Gecko
http://kids.nationalgeographic.com/animals/gecko
/#gecko-on-leaf.jpg
Learn more about where geckos live.

Wild Kratts: All About Lizards Activity
http://www.pbs.org/parents/wildkratts/activities/all
-about-lizards/
Find out how geckos can climb so well.

Index

climbing **16**
colors **10**
eggs **14**
food **12, 13, 15, 17**
hatchlings **14, 15**
scales **8**
skin **8, 9**
tails **11**
toes **16**